500 REAL DREAMS

500

REAL DREAMS

A Witch's Dream Journal

DIABLITO ORDO AL GHOUL

ISBN-13: 978-1978191679
ISBN-10: 1978191677

NOTE

The first 18 dreams listed here are from age four, through early adulthood. The following 482 dreams were recorded in two journals over the years 2013 to 2017 in an extreme act of dedication to the art of dreaming for the purpose of expanding my power as a witch and the exploration of the dream world. I have held nothing back in describing them, and this book is simply the honest account of what I have experienced in my dreams. I hope that you will see similarities between my dreams and yours, and thus, you will learn from my experience and also begin to explore the other side of reality for yourself.

–Diablito

500 Real Dreams

1. Dreamed I was at the house where I grew up at. Out in the front driveway there was a pit about the size of a small room. The walls of the pit were made of a smooth grey stone. Chained to the wall of the pit was a wolf man. He had on dark green pants and a pink shirt that buttoned up with a collar. It was night and I could see the stars up above me. I was standing in the pit beside the wolfman, I looked up at him terrified at his coal black hair and ferocious features. I tried to walk up the stone steps leading out of the pit but my shoes were slippery and so I couldn't escape.

2. Dreamed there were little demon like cats under my bed and if I tried to get off of the bed they would hiss and claw at me.

3. Dreamed my older brother was being tickled by a pig wearing clothes.

4. Dreamed I traveled alone to a different town. Everything was very poor and worn out there. I met a boy about my age and we were friends. I felt sorry for him because my house was much nicer than his and I wanted to help him because he was my friend but I didn't know what to do or say so I just talked to him and tried to be friendly. I dreamed about the boy 3 times.

5. (flying dream number 1) Dreamed I was flying at the field near the house where I was born. My method of doing this was to lie down for sleep at night and then imagine that I was at that field, standing at a particular spot in the field, moving my arms like a bird. Suddenly the

blackness would fade away and I would be at that spot, dreaming and flying. I did this many times on many nights at the exact same spot. The feeling of the wind on my skin and the sunshine up above me was incredible. I only flew for the sheer freedom of it.

6. Dreamed I was at my parents church, in one of the side rooms. There was a hole in the window of the room and I looked through it. There seemed to be a silvery metallic tunnel extending outwards away from the window and there was a man walking down the tunnel toward me. He had long black hair and blue eyes and wore a black trenchcoat. He spoke to me and his voice seemed like many voices speaking at once. He said "I am Lucifer".

7. Dreamed I was at my parents house, in my bedroom, I looked over in the dimly lit room and on a small couch there was one of the girlfriends of a man who went to my parents church. She was wearing only a nightgown and panties. She seemed to radiate a strong sexual energy and after noticing my intense desire, pulled aside her panties to show me her vagina.

8. Dreamed about a scene that I can only describe as the end of the world. War or storms had blown apart all of the buildings and people had taken the scraps and built forts. Buildings burned people were screaming, gunshots, etc.

9. (flying dream number 2) Dreamed I was flying around at my neighborhood at night, it was winter and the ice and snow on the ground sparkled. It was quiet and I simply explored and enjoyed the quiet night.

10.(flying dream number 3) Dreamed I met the Vampire Lestat and he made me into a vampire. He killed a small white dog and told me to drink it's blood. I stood there for a long time thinking about what I had become and looking at the blood dripping from the holes on the dogs neck. Then I went hunting for my first time as a vampire. My method of doing this was to go to the local shopping mall and fly up above the lights in the parking lot. When I saw someone I wanted to feed from I would drop out of the sky and sink my fangs in their neck.

11. Dreamed I was driving a car near my house at night when I suddenly realized my passenger was a vampire. His face was deathly white and he showed me his fangs. I knew that he was not a human and he seemed very evil to me. I managed to get out of the car and make a run for it with the vampire and several others like him, both male and female, chasing me through the woods. Somehow I escaped them.

12. Dreamed I was on an old sailing boat on a river in China. It was a bright sunny day and several other boats drifted slowly down the river. To my horror a man crawled out of the river onto the boat with me and he was covered in fish scales and had fish eyes.

13. (flying dream number 4) Dreamed I looked up and saw the moon. I suddenly knew I was dreaming and decided to try to fly to the moon. After flying at great speed for a long time I landed on the surface of the moon and walked around noting the areas of light and shadow. I looked out and saw the earth floating in the sky and felt homesick so I flew back to earth, landing in a field of bright green grass with yellow flowers.

14. Dreamed I found an underwater cave. I had to swim very deep to get there and as I did so a dead body floated by me. It was dark colored and rotting and it creeped me out.

15. Dreamed I was at my parents church and I saw Anton Lavey, the founder of the church of Satan. He looked at me like he knew me and

smiled an evil looking smile. He then reached his fingers into his chest and opened it up showing black veins pumping blood inside his body.

16. Dreamed a man with snake eyes was standing in my room as I was about to wake up. He was watching me sleep.

17. Dreamed I was at my brothers house and I saw a little gray alien hiding in a corner. It was somehow normally invisible to everyone but I could see it. When it realized I could see it, it got surprised and quickly crept away.

18. Dreamed I was at my grandmothers house in the living room. My grandmother was standing on the other side of the room by a lamp. The lights were low and the house was quiet. As I looked over at my grandmother I had the most peculiar sensation. I suddenly knew that my grandmother had been dead for ten years. This caused me to realize I was dreaming. I was so shocked I threw my hands in the air. I then decided that since I was dreaming, that might actually be my dead grandmother across the room as a ghost. I decided to bravely go across the room and try to talk to her departed spirit. As I walked across the room I was overcame by strange feelings of love and childhood wonder, and I forgot I was dreaming once again.

1. Dreamed my ex girlfriend D and I were laying on a bed cuddling and it felt great. Then we were riding in a nice sports car, going back to my house and talking about the future. I told her I wanted to trade my old car for a newer one. I had a nice job and I was happy and wanted to cuddle with her again.

2. Dreamed I was patiently trying to explain something special and profound to someone. KT, an old friend I am angry with, was standing beside me. I tried to ignore her, but she kept standing there trying to listen to the conversation.

3. Dreamed I was standing in front of my house. The porch of the house was wrapped in tin. When I saw this, I suddenly realized I was dreaming.

4. Dreamed that my old Golden Dawn order friend Seth B tried to stab me with some sort of a blade. I was very scared.

5. Dreamed I was hanging out with KT somewhere and we were friends again. Somehow I forgot I was angry with her. Looking back, if I would have remembered my anger towards her, I would have ignored her again.

6. Dreamed that I had stopped smoking weed for a long time. I was about to see my ex girlfriend D again. She had been through some hard times.

7. Dreamed that I met the "pickup artist" named "mystery" and a girl he was trying to get with. I ran up to him excitedly and looked at him curiously. He looked back at me like I was crazy.

8. Dreamed I was at some kind of a church meeting with my dad and Vernon P. My dad, who has been dead for years, proudly introduced me to a church member and I shook the members hand. I had traveled "a great distance" to get to this place. Somehow I knew that the scene was a dream.

9. Dreamed I was roaming around an old house and I ran into a friend I used to do yoga with named Andrea. She was in a bathroom getting undressed. I looked through a crack in the wall and saw her. She caught me and I apologized, then realized she probably didn't care because she was a stripper.

10. Dreamed I was somewhere listening to a band play a cover of the Alice in Chains song "would?" I thought it would be a great cover for my band L.H.

11. Dreamed I went to the house of my ex girlfriend D. I was looking for her, driving my very first car, the old brown one. I was in my underwear and had a massive growth of hair on my head. Her mom was there, looking out a window, she saw me arrive but would not answer the door. I drive away sad.

12. Dreamed I was 13 years old and having secret sex with my sister.

13. Dreamed I was talking to my drummer Derrick about something, while standing in the living room of my house. Whatever we spoke of made me so excited the hairs on my arms stood up. I pointed this out to him.

14. Dreamed I was at my moms church, Jimmy Bean was there. He had been converted from being a stoner and a looser, and became a pastor of some kind. I was not impressed. My Sister Alicia was there and said

Jimmy was "really on the mark" my mother was there as well.

15. Dreamed of a giant prehistoric wolf. It was far away from me at first, standing on the roof of a house in the distance. Suddenly it came towards me very fast, I was viewing it from behind a plate glass window. It came up to the window and crashed into it trying to get at me, but I was safe behind the window.

16. Dreamed my whole family sat down for a meal. This would be impossible now because they all hate each other.

17. Dreamed of a nude girl and me staring at her clitoris.

18. Dreamed of a giant silver ufo in the sky.

19. Dreamed I was talking to my father who is dead, I was telling him about the dream I had previously had where I had seen the ufo. Then we saw several flying cars moving in the sky. Suddenly I remember many other dreams where I had seen flying cars as well.

20. (flying dream number 1.) Flying around some house that I had been to before, perhaps in another life, or dream. I was naked.

21. Dreamed I was walking around somewhere with a rice crispy treat I had stolen. Then I found another one and stole it as well.

22. Dreamed I was working at Macdonalds and I thought to myself "this sucks but at least I have a job."

23. Dreamed I was under a house digging up piles of dirt. My two old aunt's, Sharon and Brenda were there working with me. The air was

moldy and it was filthy down there.

24. Dreamed I was having a long conversation with my ex girlfriends mother about my ex girlfriend D. I was telling her that she should accept me in her daughters life because I truly cared about her daughter and would have been good to her. I asked her plainly if she could do this. I was very sincere. Then suddenly while dreaming, I remembered my previous dream of digging under the house with my old aunts.

25. Dreamed I was singing with the band and my voice wouldn't work very well because it was dry.

26. Dreamed I was sitting on the edge of an embankment having a long cuddle and kissing session with Megan K or some other pretty blond girl. Suddenly a helicopter flew across the sky upside down and landed right beside us. It was a very dangerous maneuver, and a display of future technology.

27. Dreamed I was at a creek or pool and there were girls walking around in swimsuits. One of them had a bottom piece to the swimsuit that was like fisnets. It was so hot.

28. Dreamed there was a party at my brothers garage, my band was going to play. I saw my high school crush Carrie R there and her friend Katie. I wanted to ask them if they remembered me playing guitar for them 20 years before.

29. Dreamed I was at a summer camp of sorts and met a pretty girl and we kissed. For some reason no one could know about the kiss. I left the camp in a boat across a pond or lake. I could see that she had a new boyfriend standing beside her as she waved goodbye to me. I was

crushed by this.

30. Dreamed I was standing outside a rock show naked. I suddenly realized I was the entertainment for the evening and I had to go on stage and perform. I was scared as hell, but then decided "fuck it, I am going to rock."

31. (flying dream number 2.) Dreamed I was flying around a strange neighborhood at night. I was trying to find my house. I came upon a wealthy black guy who wanted me to hang out and smoke weed with him. He seemed cool but I didn't trust him so when he tried to talk to me I flew up and landed on the roof of a nearby house.

32. Dreamed I was riding in a car with a friend when suddenly he lost control of the car and we went off the road and into a ditch. Everything was ok though, no injury.

33. Dreamed I found a large group of crystals. They were so clear and perfect I wondered if they were fake.

34. Dreamed I was hanging out with ex girlfriend D.

35. (flying dream number 3) Dreamed I was hanging out with KT at an old abandoned house, as we were leaving the house, I started flying and was about 20 feet up in the air, I tried to encourage her to fly as well but she could not do it.

36. Dreamed I came downstairs and my drummer was living here, I said to him "hey, did you get off work early?"

37. Dreamed my belt was falling apart and I was worried I could not get a new one.

38. Dreamed I kissed a girl and it was very nice.

39. Dreamed I was at a summer camp, peeping into the window of the girls dorm I see them wearing thong underwear.

40. Dreamed I came to a place where my ex wife, the love of my life, was staying with some friends of hers. I introduced myself cautiously and kindly and they seemed a bit wary of me. After a time they were more friendly and me and the ex wife Kyleen got to hang out for a while.

41. Dreamed I was in an apt. building that was owned by my aunt Sharon. It was empty and there were hundreds of empty rooms there. I wandered around thinking that I had been there before. Then my dad was there and we got into an argument and started screaming at each other. I dared him to leave me alone, or strike me, I don't know why I was angry.

42. (flying dream number 4.) Dreamed I was out at the farm I grew up on. I was flying around the farm and someone handed me a long stick that we had used to push ourselves around with when we would float around the pond in an old stock tank. I flew up in the air and hurled the stick into the center of the pond like a spear, throwing it with great force.

43. Dreamed I ran into Chance Halceth, he was gay and had his boyfriend with him, a young guy wearing flashy pink sparkly clothes and rainbow make up on his face.

44. Dreamed I was somewhere working on a project and writing notes about it on a wall. My old friend graveyard Rob was there and he kept sneaking up behind me and pinning little symbols on the wall that

appeared to be from the grimorium verum, perhaps of Lucifer or Belzebuth. He was playing a joke on me, and at the same time, displaying his magic powers.

45. Dreamed my sister came into my room wearing a bathrobe. After checking to see that no one was around, I fingered, then fucked her.

46. Dreamed my sister came into my room and begged me to do something for her, she said she would do anything so I named a large amount of money, and then said "oh, and I get to fuck you". She agreed and the deal was done.

47. Dreamed I was suddenly looking at my hands and I then realized I was dreaming. I had been trying to do this for some time as an excercise in Mexican Sorcery. I became very excited. I lowered my hands and looked around me, I saw distant mountains and green fields with flowers. I went to explore them and forgot I was dreaming.

48.(flying dream number 5) Dreamed I was at an apt complex with a friend. While standing outside I realized I could fly. I decided to fly up and look in the windows of the second level of the apartments. So I flew around looking in windows. In the first there was a family. In the second window there was a man sleeping. In the third window there was a white man playing with the tits of a black woman. In the fourth window a man woke up from his sleep and noticed me. He began yelling and shined a flashlight at me.

49. Dreamed I was at my moms church scrounging for food. Somehow I got into a screaming match with her. I told her dad cheated on her, and she was stupid, and I could not stop smoking weed, and that I was damn near starving because of her and my older brothers actions. Etc.

50. Dreamed I was somewhere with my friend KT. She was complaining that she did not have enough material to start a yoga school. I thought to myself "I do but I won't teach you".

51. (flying dream number 6.) Dreamed I was at the house of my old yoga teacher, Will P. Tara from work was there. I suddenly realized I could fly and began flying around the woods. After a while I stopped flying and came down to the ground. Tara sat on my lap. Another woman was there as well and was jealous that Tara was sitting on my lap. Will arrived and I was both happy to see him, and bored with the fact that I felt I could learn no more from him.

52. Dreamed I put on some cologne that I had stolen from my friend Derrick. He smelled the cologne and was like "what is that?" He knew I had stolen from him and I was embarrassed.

53. Dreamed my son and I were running from some sort of law enforcement that drove four wheeled off road vehicles. We were crouching in the bushes and I was teaching him how to hide.

54. Dreamed my ex girlfriend D and I were friends again and had sex and it was really good sex.

55. (flying dream number 7) Dreamed I was flying around some place that was kind of like a school cafeteria. I didn't like the people there and was avoiding them by flying up by the ceiling.

56. Dreamed my mother was telling me some kind of story about when she was young and some man trying to get with her.

57. Dreamed I argued with my mother for hours. Finally I yelled at her "I will never, ever, ever be a Christian!"

58. Dreamed I was hanging out with my ex girlfriend D. I asked her how much she loved me and she said she didn't really. It hurt so bad.

59. Dreamed the electricity was back on (it had been shut off) and I was going from room to room in my house excitedly.

60. Dreamed my ex girlfriend D said she loved me, but I didn't think she really meant it.

61. Dreamed about a demon from the "goetia of Solomon" it appeared as a dark knight.

62. Dreamed I lived on a farm. There was a horse in a barn on the farm, it was night, a wild mountian lion got into the barn and attacked the horse, it clawed it up pretty bad and there was blood everywhere. I saw the mountain lion on top of the back of the horse in the stall and it was as if the horse was screaming as the mountain lion ripped into it's flesh. Me and some other farm hands picked up tools of any kind we could find and managed to scare away the lion. I was so afraid I was shaking and sweaty and felt sick in the dream.

63. Dreamed there was a mouse in my house. We were looking at each other eye to eye.

64. Dreamed I was talking to my sons mother, Janet, about something.

65. Dreamed I was trying to play the drums but I was holding the sticks the wrong way.

66. Dreamed I got back together with my daughters mom Tracy. We had great sex. Later we were discussing being faithful to each other and she asked "well could we see other people someday?" "What about

someone of a different color?" I said "well I guess, if you want, but I think my first loyalty should be to you." Also in this dream I was at some strange house listening to some people discuss a drug deal, but they didn't know I was listening. I thought about flying around and looking in windows, I remember being on the roof of the house in the darkness.

67. Dreamed I was talking to my dad about leaving his house, and just my over all frustration. I cussed my parents, told them they were assholes, and left with nothing but a set of clothes, and shoes, which were worn out.

6s. (flying dream number s) Dreamed of a huge fight between me, and my parents. I leave school a year and a half early and then find myself flying around their old familiar church, which I hate. I land on the roof of the church and taunt my father because he cannot fly as I can. Flying is very difficult, but it brings me freedom, I flap my hands and arms like a bird to fly.

69. Dreamed KT is standing beside me and I use yoga or some sort of magic power to run away at high speed.

70. Dreamed I stole some caramelized pecans from my place of work.

71. Dreamed my aunt Leah had made some home porn movies and looked good.

72. Dreamed I was having an affair with my old girlfriend Helen and her boyfriend found out. He caught us kissing.

73. Dreamed my mom was cooking some new kinds of meals on a special skillet that only heated what food touched it surface.

74. Dreamed I was smoking some pot with a few older guys, it was nug and they were talking about how good it was.

75. Dreamed I was learning something about the separation of two kinds of substances, like oil and water, or air and smoke. I understood it at the time but lost the meaning as I woke up.

76. Dreamed me and my drummer Derrick were driving my dads old van back home from a rock show. We picked up 5 beautiful girls on the way back and I started playing with the pussy of one of them and then fucking her in the back of the van while Derrick drove. Then all five girls decided they were going to come live with me and Derrick at my house. I told the girls that, since they were so outrageously beautiful, they would have to stay hidden from the guys in my rough neighborhood. I then asked Derrick if we had any guns, should we need to protect these fine ladies.

77. Dreamed I was at my brothers business, him and his shop manager Jason were having a big argument. At one point I was standing in between them keeping them from fighting.

78. (flying dream number 9) Dreamed me and my friends were smoking pot at my house. Strange people kept showing up like some girl named Tonya, and some employees from sonic. Me and some of my friends went out in the yard to see what was going on and there were signs that the end of the world was going on. There were strange swarms of gnats and buildings were on fire in the distance. There were loud bangs from the direction of my brothers house, and police sirens. I flew down to his house about two blocks distance to investigate, but then woke up.

79. Dreamed I bought, or stole a green apple from my resturant job.

80. Dreamed something about my brother Abijah, that he was young, and I needed to watch over him and protect him.

81. Dreamed I was dating Becky Riggs again and we were kissing. More than that it seemed I was starting to date again.

82. Dreamed I made some water balloons and dropped one of them on my brother on accident.

83. Dreamed I was hiding out in an abandoned building.

84. Dreamed I was at a weird grocery store.

85. Dreamed I was having secret sex with my sister. We were lying on a bed under the covers, someone came in the room but they did not realize what was going on.

86. (flying dream number 10) Dreamed I was flying around somewhere for a long time and my ex girlfriend D was there.

87. (flying dream number 11) Dreamed again I was flying around somewhere exploring an unknown area. I kept saying "I can fly!" over and over. It was awesome.

88. Dreamed I was arguing with my mother about my older brother. I said to her "he has this big house, and all this money, and control of everything, fuck that guy!"

89. Dreamed that me and my drummer Derrick were standing on the porch of my house. He said "hey would you mind if I moved out and got a house with Nicole?" I said that was fine.

90. Dreamed I was at a party of some kind and my boss from work was there. I said to get "I have had time to observe you for a while now and I think you handle stress well." she simply smiled.

91. (flying dream number 12) Dreamed I was flying around somewhere. I kept saying to my self "I am dreaming! I am flying!"

92. Dreamed about my ex girlfriend D. We talked for a long time and shared heart energy.

93. Dreamed my ex girlfriend D and I were talking for a long time, she promises not to cheat and I promise to save myself for her, we cuddle in ectasy.

94. Dreamed I was on the parking lot at Hobby Lobby. Me and my son Ashton were learning how to ski, because there was snow everywhere.

95. Dreamed I was looking out the window and I saw a semi truck pulling a greyhound bus, and another bus through the sky on an invisible road.

96. Dreamed I went back to church school and was trying to get a diploma. I was down in one of the little classrooms there getting frustrated with a mess of textbooks. Kolours Voss was there, at first she seemed a little standoffish, but after a while she started talking about how she was studying to lose her English accent.

97. Dreamed my ex girlfriend D came back and was living at my house again. I came home to her and we embraced. I was overjoyed.

98. Dreamed my son stole my truck keys and I yelled at him "how could you even think of stealing my truck keys , son? Thats pathetic!"

99. Dreamed I was running on stilts and going very fast, my son had a pair of stilts as well through and was running even faster.

100. Dreamed something about a snake, and that it was having it's fangs removed.

101. (flying dream number 13) Dreamed I was out at my old house on fountain road and I began flying. By using a special body posture I could remain in the air for long periods of time. I flew probably half a mile. I jumped off of the toof of my house and flew away.

102. (flying dream number 14) Dreamed I was flying around somewhere and discovered I could greatly alter my flight by concentrating on the area below me and "pushing" this causes me to sail through the air over vast distances.

103. Dreamed I was having secret sex with my sister and it was hot and heavy.

104. Dreamed Eva Hart walked by me last in a line of pretty girls. She was dressed in red with ornate designs on her blouse. She was still unattractive but she was trying to be pretty.

105. Dreamed I was coming down the stairs at my moms house and I saw my brother Abijah come in the front door holding a giant stuffed tiger. I jumped back at first because I did not realize the tiger was stuffed. It reminded me of the prehistoric wolf I had seen in a prevous dream.

106. Dreamed I met a young lady who was very nice and sweet and I gave her a hug. Some guy came up and accused me of kissing her and said she was too young to be kissed. I said "oh I didn't kiss her, I just

gave her a hug.

107. Dreamed that redheaded girl Faith, from work, was wearing a swimsuit.

108. Dreamed I was standing on a porch with a group of people. The porch was overhanging a small pond. My ex wife Kyleen was there and so were her two kids. I helped them with something and got to hang out with her for a while. A small alligator was swimming in the pond, my father was there and he grabbed it and threw it into a small kids pool. We did not know what to do with the alligator and debated shooting it.

109. Dreamed about Cammelia P. She justs finds me somehow.

110. Dreamed I was moving from group to group talking to different people.

111. Dreamed I was in a house that belonged to me. There was a deep, deep pit in the center of the living room. Cables had been attached to the walls of the house and by holding onto the cables, me and some other friends were able to climb out of the pit. It was a long climb, and we were glad to be out of the pit.

112. Dreamed about Amanda from work. I put my hands on her hips and almost kissed her. In my dream I thought that the word "ched" meant "to look", and so the name of the restaurant I worked at, "cheddars", meant "lookers" as in, pretty girls you want to look at.

113. Dreamed my mom was old, and nearly blind, and stranded outside my house. She had cooked a bunch of hamburgers for the illegal Mexican workers at her shop. I felt sorry that she was nearly blind, but still wanted her to get the hell off of my land and told her so.

114. Dreamed I was hanging out with my dead father and he was alive again. In my dream I saw this as that he had been gone a long time and he had came back. I told him "one of these days your going to tell me where you have been, and what you have been doing since you have been gone."

115. Dreamed someone with gentle fingers found a pimple on my jaw and was popping it. I had an "ahhh" sensation.

116. Dreamed I had decided to go back to school and get an algebra teachings that I missed. After realizing the amount of work involved I decided to move out of my parents house, and start a new life instead.

117. Dreamed something about a magic sword, I was carrying it around and some Mexican guy grabbed it from me to look at it.

118. Dreamed Mutley from the radio station called with a show for my band.

119. Dreamed my brother Abijah popped up in a doorway, with short hair and looking trendy.

120. (flying dream number 15) Dreamed I was at my moms house and Rose P was there. I gave her a hug and then flew up on the roof of the house to sneak a cigarette.

121. Dreamed someone told me my breath was bad and it hurt my feelings.

122. Dreamed I was around a lot of people at various places and it just seemed to be a drain on my energy to see what they all wanted.

123. Dreamed I was working on fixing the roof of an old trailer that I had lived in when I was a kid. I was working with someone else and when we got to the middle of the roof it was really torn. I said to the person working with me "don't be discouraged, we can do this, I have seen this before". And I had seen it, in a different dream.

124. Dreamed my sister came in my room, I made her promise not to tell and then threw her down on a bed and played with her pussy for a little while.

125. Dreamed I was talking to some pretty girl at a restaurant table and then my ex girlfriend Chevelle came up and was all "hey, what's up?"

126. Dreamed my ex girlfriend D came up and put her hands on my shoulders and kissed my neck, I sort of leaned back into her and said "your so sexy."

127. Dreamed something about my neighbor "wormy" and a girl.

128. Dreamed Rochelle and I were babysitting a little kid and when she left for a little bit, a friend of hers came up to me and said I was cute.

129. Dreamed I stuck my dick in my girlfriend, Chevelle.

130. Dreamed I was at my moms church and I wanted a cigarette, I snuck out a side door of the church and there was the pastor and several others smoking cigarettes.

131. Dreamed I was singing a song with my band called "fresh blood."

132. Dreamed I was at the mall and a cop ran by waving a gun, trying to catch another mall cop, to arrest him.

133. Dreamed I was with my sister, cleaning her room. There was a guitar there. Suddenly mom and dad came in the room and accused us of getting it on. We denied it and they left, and then we did get it on.

134. Dreamed there were 6 judges dressed in black at my house. I asked them if I had done anything wrong and they said no, so I told them to leave.

135. Dreamed I was at a party that my band had played at, it was getting wilder and wilder and there were some teenage girls making out with some older looking guys.

136. Dreamed Shannon Low was at a L.H. band practice, he sang a bit, then my band and I performed the song "blindman."

137. Dreamed I was talking to a woman from my mothers church named Gail Rinker, she told me that in her former life before joining the church,she had been a prostitute. I said to her "are you serious?" she said yes and I said "I don't judge you."

138. Dreamed I went running naked in the rain, I did not care who saw me and it was awesome. Finally I had to be around other people so I put on some underwear.

139. Dreamed I hit my mother over the head with a glass mug, knocking her unconcious. I felt terrible after I woke up and did not want to record the dream.

140. Dreamed my "farm" got stolen.

141. Dreamed I was in some sort of darkly lit city, I was travelling alone and there seemed to be a danger from street bums. I looked around me for a piece of trash to use as a weapon.

142. Dreamed everyone left my neighbor "wormys" house and wormy turned to me and pulled out a joint of weed to smoke.

143. (flying dream number 16) Dreamed I was somewhere near a large body of water, I was in a house, talking to a girl, she told me that she had a boyfriend but I wanted to play with her anyway. I told her so and then kissed her. Then I flew out the window and over the lake to the other side, where there was a large treehouse.

144. (flying dream number 17) Dreamed I was in some strange place and wanted to fly. I jumped out a window and fell down to a sandy beach below, despite my best efforts at flying. Then I was at my moms church, I ran for the door to get out of there and started flying, in the doorway. I thought wildly to myself "I did it!" I floated for a moment, then everything was ripped away as I woke up.

145. (flying dream number 18) Dreamed I was at my brother Amiels house. Flying up very high above the trees I fall down and almost crash into some power lines. I then join a group of kids playing.

146. (flying dream number 19) Dreamed I was hanging out with Miley Cyrus. I was kind of her date. Michael Jackson's family was also somehow involved in the dream. Anyway I had to transport her safely from one place to another and as she walked on the ground I flew above her as her companion and escort. There was a homeless bum walking behind her at a distance of about 30 feet. I did not know if he was a threat so I dive bombed him like a bird or airplane. At some point earlier in the dream I had picked up Miley in my arms and flew with her, I felt so powerful to be able to fly and carry her at the same time.

147. Dreamed was somewhere telling someone about flying in the previous dream and laughing about it.

148. Dreamed I was at work at Cafe Del Rio and my shoe fell off and my shoes are falling apart.

149. Dreamed I an talking to Kurt Zimmerman, the owner of a bar my band plays at. I am cleaning or organizing something or setting up for a show. Then I accidentally drop a steel bar on his head. We have a long conversation after that, that is partly me apologizing, and partly me being a smart ass.

150. Dreamed Chevelle and her gay friend "do da" were at one of my rock shoes, I was standing on the other side of Chevelle when do da gave her a hug, his hand accidentally brushed mine and I jumped back and was all "ewwww gross". (because he has aids and I didn't want him to touch me)

151. Dreamed my ex wife Kyleen and I were cuddling and I asked her if I could eat her pussy. She said yes and I said "do you remember the time we smoked a cigarette together while fucking?"

152. Dreamed Chevelle and I switched bodies and I was in her body and she was in mine.

153. Dreamed I was at my mom and dads church and my dad accused me of being drunk, which I was not. I told him so and then got the hell out of there.

154. (flying dream number 20) Dreamed the most powerful flying dream ever! I was flying around my mom and dads farm and there were a couple guys there I did not like. I started flying above them taunting

them and then discovered to my suprise that they could fly as well. They started chasing me all through the sky and around the farm. I was scared so I flew faster and farther than ever before.

155. (flying dream number 21) Dreamed that I remembered my flying dream from the night before and tried to fly as fast and as far. I couldn't do it as well this time, because I was not afraid of anything at that time.

156. Some skanky girl that had a crush on me tried to kiss me and I was like "ewwww get away."

157. Dreamed I escaped from some kind of prison camp.

158. Dreamed I was explaining to someone about my family situation and how I must be poor to be free from my family.

159. Dreamed I argued and fought terribly with a little asian girl.

160. (flying dream number 22) Dreamed I was at my moms church and had a big argument with her and my sister. After telling them to fuck off I flew around the church in a giant circle and came back down to land on the back parking lot.

161. Dreamed I completely remodeled my house, I walked around admiring the garden and stone water pools I created in the yard. "Now my family can see how well I am doing, and get mad" I thought.

162. Dreamed me and someone else went over to the house of this preppy guy from work named "Parker". The person I was with got nervous and left but I didn't care who he was or thought he was and so I stayed and met his family.

163. (flying dream number 23) Dreamed I was flying and had great control of it. I was flying around my neighborhood and travelled in the air from my aunt's house to mine.

164. (flying dream number 24) Dreamed I was at mom and dads house and there was a tree house on the back of their house. I climed up in the tree house, and then jumped out of it and started flying around the farm, waving, yelling, and doing the "moonwalk" through the air as my older brother and father watched. My dad said "why don't you come down here and help me change the oil filter on this forklift before the weekend." I considered for a moment if I was dreaming, but then decided I was awake and was using my real body to fly.

165. Dreamed I was in the courtyard of the park apartments. Cliff was there, I told him he was a fuck off for not helping sell tickets to the rock show the band was set up to play at.

166. Dreamed I saw my old yoga teacher Will P. He was working for his business, and unloading a portable barn he had built off the back of a truck he was driving. I stopped to see him and He was smoking a cigarette, which he does not do. We talked for a while about addiction.

167. Dreamed there was a basement in my house. This is the second time I have had the dream. This time I was not scared to go down there and look and see what was there. I explored the basement, and took my mother and stepbrother Ricardo down there. There were lights on, and a radio playing that had been on for years, but idk how I knew this. Plus there were a lot of strange junk objects that had been there for years. I Decided I was going to remodel the basement.

168. Dreamed I was sick and almost puked in front of some people I knew.

169. Dreamed my neighbor Wormy and his son half worm were here at the house looking for weed, I said I didn't have any and mentioned the names of two neighborhood dealers they might check with.

170. Dreamed I was at some "mega church" and there was a little kid there playing, perhaps my daughter. I was trying to take care of the kid. Somehow I found a stash of old porn. I wanted to look at it but felt guilty because I did not want the kid to see the porn. Then I met a talking lion that was having a struggle sounding out words. Then I met the pastor of the church "the crystal cathedral" he was trying to write a sermon on some new type of computer.

171. Dreamed I was working for my brother Amiel again. I was down at his house and he was showing me a guitar he had. I picked it up and started playing some metal riffs. We talked about the guitar for a moment. In a moment of friendliness I forgot I hated him and said "hey do you know I get to open the show for the band Drowning Pool in a few weeks?" He was shocked.

172. Dreamed that my house was a macdonalds restaurant. I worked at the resturant with my mother and sister. When the resturant got really busy, both of them simply quit working and left me to run the drive through by myself. My mother and sister calmly refused to do any work as I ran around frantically and everything went to hell. I grew more and more frantic and started screaming at my mother and sister. My mother gathered a few children around her and started having a bible study, she looked at me as if she was concerned I was freaking out.

173. Dreamed I was riding in a car with KT. We went to see my ex girlfriend D. When we found her she acted hurt and said she didn't want to see me. Then I was riding with her in her white car and it was breaking down. I asked her why she did not have her rich parents fix it

for her and she said she had not seen then in a couple years.

174. Dreamed I was hanging out with a couple guys in my neighborhood. They were talking about killing one of their friends but I talked them out of it.

175. (flying dream number 25) Dreamed me and three other kids were out in the desert at some kind of festival and a truck came by with a ufo on the back. I became so excited I lost my ability to speak. I pointed at the ufo and tried to get the attention of the other kids. It was small and flat, and shaped like a V. I ran to where it was being unloaded and watched a man get in it and fly it up into the sky until it disappeared into the horizon. Me and the kids took off walking and came up on a house that was square and covered in dirt so it was not noticed, yet it was a very large house, probably three stories high, yet square. After a while we found a window and went inside, we found that many people lived there and there was a large amount of books. In one room there was a tree of life diagram, in the exact form I have at my house, which is different than others. I was very shocked by this. I once again felt so excited I could not breathe. Me and the other kids tried to leave the house, but the front door was locked. Then a small group of men showed up at the house, they seemed concerned about what we had seen at the house. I told them we thought the place was empty, and we hadnt broken anything. They told us to go up on the roof and wait While they decided what to do. I went up on the roof, there were a few other kids there. They knew about the house, they said it had secrets, including the secrets of ufo technology. We watched a small flying car moving around in the sky. I told the kids, "you know about this secret technology, let me show you another kind of secret power". Then I jumped off of the roof and flew around a little bit and then came back and landed on the roof. The kids were amazed. Then suddenly my form disintegrated and I woke up. Note, after I woke up in this manner I was dizzy and felt like it was hard to reform and hold my particles together, it seemed like I had just teleported and was still coming back

together.

176. Dreamed I was walking somewhere and I saw a woman with pale white skin and red hair. I stopped to get a closer look and realized it was my mother. I just kept walking and ignored her.

177. Dreamed I was somewhere with my mom and sister and my mom demanded that I guard something for her. I told her, it was the last time I would do anything for her and when I was done, that was the last time I would see her.

178. Dreamed something about riding a four wheeled vehicle though a dark and dangerous area. My son Ashton was there and I was trying to help him with something.

179. Dreamed I was talking to someone about tarot, and also calling it Rota.

180. Dreamed I was at my mothers business, the one she got from dad when he died, Jwp. She hired me to build a room there for my daughter, I was actually excited to have some work, and also to build the room for my daughter Hazel.

181. Dreamed my band was working with me at one of my jobs and people were asking me about them.

182. (flying dream number 26) Dreamed I had on a superman costume and I could fly. I was in California at a shopping mall and I wanted to go home. I had a plan to sell my house and buy a church to live in, but I did not think I could fly all the way from California to Missouri. So I had to wait for my family to give me a ride home. I told my mother that as soon as I got home I was selling My house and they would

never see me again. I wanted to fly home but it was too far. I was sad. I flew around a lot but no one knew me and I didn't know anyone. Everyone thought I was superman and I felt so alone and with no family. But I could fly.....

183. Dreamed I was in an awesome cave, it had a wooden, log like structure inside and I wondered if I could start a business in there.

184. Dreamed I was in some awful place, like a prison camp, there was this gang of terrible people there and they were going to rape some poor woman. I was trying to save her, when all seemed lost, and all hope was gone, my sons mother Janet arrived out of the blue. I pleaded with her to save us, and somehow, by wispering something into the ear of one of the men, she did. I woke Up with a great feeling of relief at having escaped certain doom.

185. Dreamed I went to Tulsa to start a new life. I was working for my father and older brother Amiel and every thing was confusing. I just wanted to go home to my real friends.

186. Dreamed I was at some kind of church camp where no one knew me, or that I was a witch. I was with some teenage girl who was cuddling up to me. I thought to myself "this is nice, I can get more pussy than I thought, wherever I go".

187. Dreamed Tracy wanted me to fuck her again, I was happy about that because that made three girls that wanted me to fuck them.

188. Dreamed I was listening to two co workers, Carol Jane and Heather, talk about me. Somehow I was in the room with them but they did not see me.

189. Dreamed a male voice called my name so loudly I thought someone was in my house. I sat up in bed and said "hello?" then I realized I did not know if I was awake or sleeping.

190. Dreamed about looking at a picture of my daughter, as I looked at the picture it changed, almost as if it were a small movie screen. I could seen it change to look like her ancestors going back into time.

191. Dreamed my phone broke in half but was still connected by a wire, I tried all kinds of ways to fix it, and there were bizarre images on the screen.

192. Dreamed I was somewhere with Rochelle, she was naked and looked amazing, it took my breath away, she smiled, I stepped closer to her and then woke up.

193. Dreamed I was talking to a girl I liked, but I had a cold and was embarrassed.

194. Dreamed I came upon my dad smoking a cigarette. I was suprised and asked him about it but he didn't answer and seemed tense. He was cleaning up the old brown trailer my family had lived in at one time. I asked him of he needed help and he said no, and then said maybe. So I started helping him and looking for things that might interest me as we cleaned. I found several occult books and a few small things I liked. This part of the dream seemed to carry on for hours. My mother arrived and I demanded that she tell me the truth about everything and as usual she was full of lies and half truths. Mom and dad argued very badly and I wanted to leave. There was a little camper trailer that I owned In the woods and I went there.

195. Dreamed I was supposed to play guitar for the band Korn. I was

scared as hell, but then I asked myself "do I have the skill to do This? Well, yes I do".

196. Dreamed I was at a family reunion and I met a man who had served in the military. I was very emotionally moved as I thanked him for his service and shook his hand.

197. Dreamed I was at Wal-Mart's, but I knew I was dreaming. I walked through the various isles looking at all the objects and it seemed so real. Yet I knew it was a dream.

198. Dreamed I told my brother there was no way I could stop smoking pot to work for his company. So he gave me a job where I made 50 dollars a day doing something for his company. Yet I was always scared he was going to take it away.

199. Dreamed something about making my own ninja weapons.

200. Dreamed I found a stash of porn and wanted to look at it, but did not because there was other people around.

201. Dreamed that I was in a trailer that was once rented out by a man named Steve Ward. My dad and older brother Amiel were there and my older brother Amiel tried to kill me. I got out of there fast.

202. Dreamed I was hanging out with someone and we found a large red and black spider.

203. Dreamed that the aunt of my ex girlfriend D was walking with a cane or walker.

204. Dreamed I was several different people.

205. Dreamed I was running up a wall and then floating in the air.

206. Dreamed I was at my brother Amiels house. I had to squeeze through a door that was too small to get inside.

207. Dreamed I was getting my dick sucked by three playboy models.

208. (flying dream number 27) Dreamed I was in some large barn demonstrating my power of flying to someone.

209. (flying dream number 28) Dreamed I was at my parents old house showing someone how to fly.

210. Dreamed I had a long talk with Stripper Andrea about her boyfriend Baxter.

211. Dreamed Eva H tried to say hi to me and said something stupid.

212. Dreamed I caught my dad fucking my sister Alicia in the tall grass next to my childhood home. They did not know I saw them and I felt weird and disgusted.

213. Dreamed Dan the man, the life regenerator on YouTube had a hot blond girlfriend and the three of us were swimming in a small pool made out of a farm stock tank.

214. Dreamed I was at an apartment and some people showed up to do a drug deal, they were driving a golf cart and arguing with each other.

215. Dreamed I was lying in bed and suddenly my ex girlfriend Chevelle was here, I thought about fucking her, then she changed into my ex girlfriend D and crawled into bed with me naked. Then I woke up suddenly and realized it was a spirit (Lilith)playing with me.

216. Dreamed I was somewhere talking about sorcery to stripper Andrea.

217. (flying dream number 29) Dreamed I was at mom and dads old trailer and I flew down the hall and across the living room. I then turned to someone and said "did you see that? I just flew" I thought I was in my body, I said "I fly all the time in dreams, but I am solid now". Once again the flight was accomplished by holding a particular body position.

218. (flying dream number 30) Dreamed I was in the back bedroom of a house and my son was there, he was complaining about something, I then flew out the window.

219. Dreamed I was working hard at an Italian resturant. My brother Abijah was there, I yelled at him for not helping me.

220. Dreamed I was riding in a car with Stripper Andrea, my ex girlfriend D and one of my kids, I was explaining something powerful to Andrea and she started to hug me, I was driving and worried I would wreck. I made a joke about her being a vampire.

221. Dreamed I was lying on my bed and looking at the ceiling. There was writing on the ceiling. I couldn't tell if I was awake or dreaming and so I directed my concentration to my eyelids and could feel them closed. By this I determined I was dreaming. I tried to read the writing but the effort made me wake up.

222. (flying dream number 31) Dreamed I was at a strange house. I didn't know anyone There, but I was demonstrating my power of flying to them.

223. (flying dream number 32) Dreamed I was at my parents church. I put my son infant son in a backpack and flew around with him on my back.

224. Dreamed Tracy and I got back together, we were happy and kissed passionately.

225. Dreamed I was going to an underground dance party.

226. Dreamed I was at a trailer and there was a man there buying drugs from my ex girlfriend Megan. She had lost weight and looked good. There was a guy there that seemed to be her boyfriend.

227. Dreamed I was somewhere with Zane and he kissed a girl. I said "wait a minute Zane, aren't you with Rochelle?" He said no.

228. Dreamed I was in a house that had a wall in the living room. I climbed over the wall and my ex girlfriend D was There, lying on a couch.

229. (flying dream number 33) Dreamed I was hanging out with my dad and I flew around his old shop.

230. Dreamed I was somewhere near my witch friend Lana and I wanted to go visit her.

231. Dreamed I was at a mega church and exploring it's halls and

stairways.

232. Dreamed I was somewhere and this big black guy was sexually harrassing the women there.

233. Dreamed Baxter asked me for a cookie in the refrigerator.

234. (flying dream number 34) Dreamed I flew up a long road that led up to the too of a hill. I turned around and looked how far I had flown and was amazed.

235. (flying dream number 35) Dreamed I was at an apt. complex owned by my aunt Sharon. There was a bunch of people downstairs working in a kitchen. I came in the house like a ninja then flew upstairs. A girl came in the house looking for me, she had a very small mouth like D. Then I realized it was my ex girlfriend D and kissed her.

236. Dreamed I saw my old drummer Jess J walking down the road, I didn't want to give him a ride in my car but I did anyway because I felt obligated.

237. (flying dream number 36) Dreamed I was a a strange place where there were some people cooking dope. I fly around and escape from them, there was also some kids there and I taught them how to fly.

238. Dreamed about the sigils from the Goetia, one of them had a flag waving on the side of it.

239. (flying dream number 37) Dreamed I was flying around various places looking in the windows of houses and seeing people go about their lives.

240. Dreamed about an end of the world type scene where everyone was divided into gangs and defending our territory with darts from a dart board.

241. (flying dream number 38) Dreamed I was flying around and met a beautiful asian girl. I taught her how to fly and we flew together by touching hands. I wispered to her "this is what I have always wanted".

242. Dreamed I was back together with Tracy and we were at a summer camp. One of her ex boyfriends showed up and I had to leave at the same time. I leaned over to her and whispered "you are not going to hook up with him are you?". She said no, but I knew she would.

243. Dreamed my sister came in my room and I said "we haven't fucked in a long time, lets fuck".

244. (flying dream number 39) Dreamed I flew in front of my brothers daughter, Grace. She was surprised and said "you can fly!" I said "yeah I have been flying for years and no one believes me".

245. (flying dream number 40) Dreamed I saw a beautiful redheaded girl and flew up to the second story window of her house to look at her.

246. Dreamed I almost drank out of a cup someone had spit in.

247. (flying dream number 41) Dreamed I was flying, using a blanket held in my hands like a parachute.

248. Dreamed I was wearing a shirt with the band name Type O Negative and someone was trying to look at it.

249. (flying dream number 42) Dreamed I was flying and gliding around somwhere and showing people that I could fly.

250. Dreamed I was driving a little red go-cart at work.

251. Dreamed something about my sister Alicia.

252. Dreamed I took Lana (the old witch friend of mine) some medicine after her husband Tim had died.

253. Dreamed someone called my sister a bitch and I threatened to beat them with the handle of a mop.

254. Dreamed I saw my old friend George Rollins. I was like "hey man! Long time!".

255. (flying dream number 43) Dreamed I was at the farm I grew up on. It was very windy. I was trying to fly in the wind and couldn't do it very well. I decided to build a wingsuit.

256. Dreamed I was getting beaten by my father, I was struggling against him, and trying to draw attention to what was going on but no one noticed.

257. Dreamed I was going to fuck my sister.

258. Dreamed I saw my ex girlfriend Chevelle and suddenly there was a snake and a cat in the room.

259. Dreamed I had a "Farm" and my products were very large.

260. Dreamed I saw a girl I know and thought to myself "the only reason why I would try to talk to her is to invite her to my rock show or fuck her".

261. Dreamed about a dead mouse in a mousetrap, and about another mouse with all white hair.

262. Dreamed that I was lighter than other people and I wondered if I could fly.

263. Dreamed I found a pick to dig with. I thought "this is just what I needed", and took it to my front yard.

264. (flying dream number 44) Dreamed I was somewhere flying, I barely remember it now, but I do remember I went up very high and came down quickly.

265. Dreamed about a set of magical tools with little stars on them, they were similar to golden dawn tools but slightly different. I also had a set of golden dawn magic tools as well in the dream.

266. Dreamed I met a guy my co workers at the drywall business talk about often. His name was OT.

267. Dreamed I saw a tornado. It was awesome to look at, but I decided I needed to take shelter.

268. (flying dream number 45) Dreamed I was flying around somewhere in a dimly lit city. My friend Cliff was there and I thought he was going to get attacked by some people. I tried to help him by attacking the people who were bothering him. I tried to fly as fast as I had in a different dream where I was in a battle with two people, but the effort

of flying so fast woke me up.

269. Dreamed I met my ex wife kyleen again. I kissed her. The place where we were at was a place I have been to before in dreams but never in the physical world.

270. Dreamed I was having secret sex with my sister in the trailer we lived in growing up. We almost got caught but did not. Someone was watching television on the other end of the trailer while this was going on.

271. Dreamed my brother Amiel called me on the phone and asked me how I was doing. I said "I have a job in drywall and I smoke weed, if you don't like it, fuck off".

272. Dreamed someone found my warm, grey, stocking cap.

273. (flying dream number 46) Dreamed I was flying out at moms house.

274. Dreamed I was in the attic of the barn, on the farm I grew up on.

275. Dreamed I saw one of the Olsen twins, or someone who looked like them. They were smiling at me as I woke up.

276. Dreamed I was driving my truck home from work and it was kind of sputtering and I thought "omg I need money".

277. Dreamed I was looking at some drywall mud on a wall, some of it was smooth and some of it was rough.

278. Dreamed I found some porn magazines, I decided to take them

outside and burn them in a barrel. As I went outside I saw Cliff standing on the porch. I turned away so I didn't look at him, I was so disgusted with his drug use.

279. Dreamed I had two glass slides used to play guitar with, one was thick, and the other was thin.

280. Dreamed my sister Alicia tried to walk into my house. I became enraged and told her I would grab her by the hair and drag her outside of she did not knock before coming in my house.

281. Dreamed I was driving across a vast frozen lake.

282. Dreamed I was having a conversation with a group of girls, and guys about relationship equality.

283. (flying dream number 47) Dreamed I was flying somewhere, idk where but I couldn't forget it.

284. Dreamed my mom was on my porch in a car. I stuck my head out the front door and looked at her, then simply shrugged and went back inside.

285. Dreamed I was in the golden dawn again. I was at a temple and the energy and peace and power was so profound it made me be in awe of it. I realized once again that I am and shall always be a golden dawn adept.

286. Dreamed Cliff and some of his junkie friends came to my house. I told them to go away and threatened them with a stick.

287. Dreamed I passionately kissed a girl.

288. (flying dream number 48) Dreamed I was hanging out with some pretty girls and there was a ledge nearby. I slyly waited until they were watching me and then jumped off the ledge. Instead of falling as they thought I would I started flying around and surprised them, much to my satisfaction.

289. Dreamed I was hanging out with some guys from work and the boss showed up. He wanted to draw something on my hand.

290. Dreamed I was at a place that used to be a golden dawn temple. There was carpet on the floor, but there were the traditional black and white tiles underneath it.

291. Dreamed I got a pet bear. I was playing with it on the floor of my grandmothers house. I felt an incredible amount of affection for the bear and was rolling around on the floor wrestling with it. I was talking to it like a baby calling it a "hunk of bear". The bear was like a big fuzzy bean bag that kept rolling around on top of me.

292. Dreamed I got some various kinds of ninja stars.

293. Dreamed an extremely long dream. I did so many things in the dream it seemed like I lived a whole different life. Also I fucked my sister and she loved it. This is really strange to me. I don't spend time thinking about this in waking life, but it happens a lot in the dream world. It seems so natural there, so passionate.

294. Dreamed I saw my sister naked.

295. Dreamed me and my kids were out at my parents farm. Dad came

riding up on a motorcycle and some men in a geep were chasing him. He was riding fast and they were shooting at him. He circled the house a few times and then jumped off the motorcycle and started running. I felt tremendous fear as I watched all this and then the men shot my father. I told my mother to go into the trailer and get a gun. By the time she did that, the shooters were upon our hiding spot. I kept hoping my mother would have the nerve to shoot them but she seemed paralyzed with fear.

296. Dreamed I was at a place where there was a social scene. Kolours Voss was there and she climbed on my lap and started kissing me and rubbing her crotch on me.

297. (flying dream number 49) Dreamed I was teaching Keith's kids about magic and showing them I could fly. I was able to remain motionless in the air for long periods of time and demonstrated this power right in front of them. I was giving them a talk about secrecy in magic when I woke up, I said "if I give you a document on magic, and tell you to keep it secret, you must keep It secret, even from your own mother".

298. Dreamed about Tracy's boyfriend Cliff C. I met him somewhere and tried to ask him to forgive me for the wrongs he thought I did. Finally we shook hands and were cool.

299. (flying dream number 50) Dreamed I was hanging out with a bunch of kids I knew and teaching them to fly.

300. Dreamed I saw a man driving a car, wearing a ski mask.

301. Dreamed I was at the old mining pit near my childhood farm. The place where the dirt was blue. There was a lake there and people were

swimming in the water on a sunny day. I was holding on to a tree branch and my sister swam up and started talking to me.

302. Dreamed the lake in the previous dream was filled in with all the blue dirt around it. One of the hills was left and it had a cave in it and it was filled with speakers and musical gear. There was so much musical equipment there, and somehow I knew that no one else knew it was there, it was like a magic cave filled with treasures for me. I decided to steal just one guitar amp for my band and was in the process of doing so when a police car drive down the nearby road. I did not get caught.

303. Dreamed I was trying to read a contract that was for the sale of my truck, but I couldn't because it was in Spanish.

304. Dreamed I saw my mother, she was young and beautiful and wearing modern tightfitting clothes like she would never wear in real life. She hugged a handsome young man.

305. Dreamed I had been at my moms church and then left, there was a Christian guy from the church who followed me home, I realized that he didn't belong around me and told him he had no right to follow me.

306. Dreamed Geo R had a job at Gringos resturant and I was working there as well.

307. Dreamed a couple girls liked me and one of them kissed me.

308. Dreamed my ex girlfriend Chevelle, and her daughter and some other girl were all lying around me on a bed or couch and being really cuddly and nice to me.

309. Dreamed of my ex wife Kyleen, she was living in a house with KT, in a backroom with a plastic sheet over the door tacked on with pushpins. She was playing guitar and singing in the way she always used to do. I told her I wanted to play a song for her and at first she said no, but I was very sincere, so she came to the door of the room and talked to me for a while. I told her she was so beautiful and she smiled in a wonderful way and gave me a hug. I woke up and cried I was so moved emotionally.

310. Dreamed a very long dream where me and some other people were kidnapped. We were all very afraid and there was extreme tension in the air. After a long time, somehow the tables were turned on the kidnappers and athough one of the escaped, the other one was beaten to death.

311. Dreamed about a guy that had a restaurant built into a tiny camper that he was living in. He also had some broken down electronics. I sort of felt sorry for the guy and so I borrowed some of the electronics and gave him some money in case I could not return. I basically planned to throw the electronics away and leave him the money as a gift.

312. Dreamed about someone playing "enter sandman" by Metallica on bass and me watching them and offering guidance.

313. Dreamed my shoes were old and worn out and I was worried I wouldn't have money to get new ones.

314. Dreamed I was serving at a restaurant and someone ordered a drink called a "vegetarian proverb".

315. Dreamed I had two jobs and I was worried I was forgetting one of

them.

316. Dreamed about two old guys in my neighborhood. "Big Rob" was trying to be friends with Steve S., but Steve wouldn't forgive him for an old argument between them.

317. Dreamed my brothers wife had gotten pregnant from her affair and she was ashamed. It had something to do with a picture in my brothers office.

318. Dreamed something about my ex girlfriend D. We were talking again.

319. Dreamed I got a tooth knocked out and was embarrassed for people to see me.

320. Dreamed I was late on my truck payment and Steve came to repo it.

321. Dreamed Steve S. was making wine from peaches.

322. Dreamed Stephanie Hardesty from my old job at the olive garden came looking for me and found me and told me she had been waiting for me and that she wanted to be my girlfriend.

323. Dreamed I was at a meeting at my moms church and there were hot teenage girls running around in their panties. It was driving me wild! I could not believe my eyes!

324. Dreamed I ran into Russ Milar at a party and said hello.

325. Dreamed I was at my brothers shop, he tried to talk to me and I said "I don't really want to talk to you, were not friends".

326. (flying dream number 51) Dreamed I was flying at my moms church. I was trying to escape some one who was chasing me.

327. Dreamed I was walking by my brothers house at night. I could hear him and his wife yelling at each other. I contemplated sneaking up closer to the house to listen to the conversation but decided against it.

328. Dreamed I was having a conversation with my mother and she was going on and on about nothing. I said "there is no point in small talk". Some unknown man was there with her, he seemed to have a feeling about him that indicated he was my moms church friend, someone who agreed with her completely. He tried to hit me on the head and I jumped on him like an animal and told him I would poison him, and "fuck him up" if he messed with me.

329. Dreamed my dad was physically very rough with me and I decided to grind up one of the seeds from the datura plant and put it in his drink to punish him.

330. Dreamed I was watching some children including Ashton and Hazel. The kids ran off in different directions and I was running around trying to find them. I found Ashton and Josh, hiding under a piece of cardboard out on a parkinglot somewhere and told them it was very bad of them to run away and I couldn't find their sister. I then woke up in a panic.

331. Dreamed I helped a guy start his car at a convenience store by pushing it. Then a fight broke out between some rough looking people but I stayed away from it.

332. Dreamed I had........travelled a long way. I met these two girls who seemed to be really good friends of mine. Somehow I spent time thinking about how it was a strange thing to have met these two girls, because the world was so big, and they were such good friends.

333. Dreamed I ate one and a half hits of acid given to me by a "friend" of my daughter.

334. Dreamed I saw Andy Cornett. He had gotten out of prison and I gave him a hug.

335. Dreamed I was at this old house at a party and I accidentally saw the breasts of Natalie Ward and they were very nice.

336. Dreamed I was in the yard of a poor Mexican house and there was some guy talking excitedly about a flying chicken, I even saw the damn thing, flying around in the dimly lit sky. It felt like this dream had something to do with Don Juan and the Toltec Sorcerers.

337. Dreamed I was teaching a yoga class and there was a little girl that liked me, she smiled at me and came over to do yoga beside me and had cute tiny little toes.

338. Dreamed I was at a piano recital where a lot of kids were performing, including myself. Everyone was nervous. Someone wished me luck.

339. Dreamed I was at a house where a group of people were sleeping on couches and on the floor. It was time to wake up and it was my job to wake everyone up so I was going around from person to person gently shaking them on the shoulders.

340. Dreamed I was at a church youth camp and my sister arrived. I told her "lets blow off this church camp and go somewhere and fuck". We went back to out hotel but there were other church members around so nothing happened.

341. (flying dream number 52) Dreamed I was out at an old barn and when the wind blew very hard I could use ninja powers of the mind to let the wind lift me up in the air and fly. Someone else was there and saw me.

342. Dreamed my brother Amiel stole some pages from the book I am writing on magic (liber al ghoul). I chased him and pulled his hair to get them back.

343. Dreamed I was under the influence of mandrake root and was having sex. I had the most mind blowing orgasm and came a huge load of semen.

344. Dreamed I was mixing a recipie of herbs into a cauldron on a fire outdoors. Someone was teaching me the recipie at first, and then I accomplished it on my own. It seemed like I was cooking, or making witches flying ointment.

345. Dreamed I saw someone leading the pornstar Gauge into a room to do a porn scene.

346. Dreamed an extremely vivid dream with Shannon Low in it, he was selling weed and it looked like he might get busted. There were these two remarkable people there, they seemed Hindu, or something similar, I couldn't place where they were from. A guy and a girl.

347. Dreamed a wierd dream of having sex with my sister again when

my father was not around. Lots of emotion, very intense.

348. Dreamed I was at my moms church and there was a mountain lion on the loose in the church.

349. Dreamed Tracy and I got back together as a couple. She got out of the bathtub and was naked underneath a nightgown that had slits in it and was very sexy. We talked about our daughter and I said that I loved both of them. Then a couple of friends came over and we were going to play a game of cards. It seemed like a normal day in our lives.

350. Dreamed I was standing out in the yard at night talking to a friend of mine. A huge ufo appeared in the sky, it was glowing white with arm like things that came out of it. It seemed to float down close to the ground and spray the vegetation with a sort of glowing purple powder. Lights shined out of the ufo as it released the powder. Me and my friend observed the object and talked about it.

351. Dreamed I was in an old theatre talking with a group of friends. There were dozens of people all around talking normally. Suddenly a large red and orange dragon came through the door and started breathing fire and destroying everything. I was so scared all I could do was run through a side door and up a flight of stars. There was a girl with me running from the dragon. When we got to the top of the stairs the stairway opened up to a balcony that overlooked the theatre. The dragon was on the floor eating someone and the whole place was burned and there were charred, dead bodies everywhere. The dragon saw us and came at us with a fury. We escaped through another door and hid under a stairway outside the building, under a blanket. At any moment the dragon might find us and it would mean certain death. Yet somehow it did not.

352. Dreamed I was taking a piss in a factory somewhere, in a urinal

and my piss was dark yellow and full of toxins that were being purified out to pass a drug test.

353. Dreamed I was on stage at the blackthorn bar performing the song "the vampire" with my band. Carrie Raleigh was there and I put my arm around her as I sang.

354. Dreamed I was telling Cliff that I was not happy he had stolen my copy of the book "Liber Lilith" by Donald Tyson.

355. Dreamed I was practicing martial arts moves with my neighbors sai weapons.

356. Dreamed I got a job at this mom and pop style restaurant and then I realized I couldn't work there because it was 45 minutes drive from my house and the pay was only minimum wage lol. There was some pretty blond girl there and we were holding hands and talking about being together.

357. (flying dream number 53) Dreamed I showed some guy I could fly, I said "do you want to see a real magic trick?" "watch this" then I levitated in front of him. Later, in the same dream I walked across the room of my parents trailer while remaining about six inches off the ground. I then told the guy I was talking to that I had gone invisible by using magic, but that it was not easy, and that I could not do it all the time.

358. Dreamed I was somewhere where there were baby goats being born. They nibbled on my fingers like baby goats do.

359. Dreamed my dad bought a huge house out in the country, it used to be a call center and had large rooms.

360. Dreamed I sang some songs from my metal band at my moms church. I had no drummer or bass guitar player with me but I did a good job anyway.

361. Dreamed about my ex girlfriend D. She was at the bandroom walking around naked and sat down next to my guitarist. I was angry at this and told her she was being a slut and to get the fuck out of there. Later in the dream we were talking and getting close again.

362. Dreamed my brother Abijah was going on and on about the lyrics to various Rammstien songs.

363. Dreamed I was driving down a road and I saw a truck in front of me that appeared to be full of stuff from someone who was moving. A strap broke on the truck so I flagged them down to tell them. Inside the truck was a single mom with an adorable little daughter. They were both very nice and friendly and I jokingly said I would like to take the daughter home with me to raise as my own.

364. Dreamed I was at my moms church and two latino guys came in to rob the place. They came up to me and one of them put a gun against my spine. The only way I could think of to keep them from shooting me was to say they were cowards for having guns and challenge to fight one in a fair fight with fists. Kyleens children were there and I was scared for them.

365. Dreamed I was sort of getting back with Tracy. We lived in a trailer across from my dads shop and dad was still alive. He was riding a motorcycle around and had a couple grandkids on the back with him. My daughter Hazel was still a kid in the dream.

366. Dreamed I was driving the silver Ford Ranger I lost to repo, on my

way to work.

367. Dreamed I was hanging out at the house with some friends who were magicians. I went to the back room and looked out a window into the night. Suddenly I saw Eva H looking in the window at me spying. She was wearing a jet black dress or magic robe. It was impressive. She had her make up all done well and was radiating a lot of power. She got scared when I saw her and ran for her car which was parked up the road. She was clumsy but fast for a girl of her size. I was very impressed. She seemed to have her magic with her strongly.

368. Dreamed about moms church and finding a bunch of magic mushrooms there and hiding them from the cops.

369. Dreamed about a large vine that I was swinging on like Tarzan.

370. Dreamed I had a pretty new girlfriend but I caught her cheating on me. Also I dreamed my mom was watching "the vampire Lestat on tv. (that would never happen lol)

371. Dreamed the girl Diacylene from work was talking to me and touching my hand in a very gentle way. There was a tremendous transfer of energy between us. Then me, her and two others were hanging out in a bathtub. I tried to lay my head on her lap but she brushed me away. I don't know why, I just wanted to feel that sense of closeness again. Then the alarm went off and I woke up. I thought to myself, in my waking state, "I wonder what my ex girlfriend Chevelle is doing right now?" I then fell asleep again and dreamed I was standing outside a trailer and I saw Chevelle coming out the door of the trailer and walking down some steps. It was a brightly lit day in the dream. I looked at her once more, then woke up again.

372. Dreamed I found an extra room in my house, in between the bathroom and back bedroom. I wanted to put a hidden door on it and make it a secret room, it had a cool place for a bookshelf. Somehow my mom was at my house and saw the room.

373. Dreamed I had sex with some girl I never met before in the physical world.

374. Dreamed I saw some teens watching porn and I was kind of concerned about it.

375. (flying dream number 54) Dreamed I was at an insane asylum and I was a patient there. I didn't like it there and tried to fly up in the air to escape the place. I couldn't fly very well and felt heavy. I convinced one of the other patients there to boost me up on the roof so I could try to fly again and build up more speed and energy to escape the walled in area of the asylum.

376. Dreamed I was at a party at the band room. People were like "oh there is Arundell, he never gets out of the house". Shannon Low was there.

377. (flying dream number 55) Dreamed I was on the porch of a trailer my aunt and uncle used to live in. There was a man there I was teaching how to fly. I completely knew I was dreaming. I kept telling the man I was talking to "were dreaming right now! You don't realize this but we are dreaming right now!" It was so awesome, complete lucidity. I then saw Cammelia P and pulled her into the sky. After a while she could fly as well and we flew together.

378. (flying dream number 56) Dreamed I was flying around very fast and well by shooting energy out of my feet. My ex wife's son Henry

was there. He looked about 16 and had long hair like he was in a band.

379. Dreamed I was at a busy work scene. Jason Stark was there, I yelled at him. Them I was at another work scene yelling at my one time boss Tommy Harper.

380. Dreamed Tracy showed me herself naked.

381. Dreamed I realized I was dreaming and was excitedly tellin other people "you don't know it but your dreaming!"

382. Dreamed Chevelle and I were arguing and she finally forgave me and we hugged.

383. Dreamed I was in a warehouse doing a job that I liked and was happy.

384. Dreamed I ran into one of the members of the golden dawn order I once belonged to. His name was Frater IC. We talked about the old temple of Ptah and of the Al Ghoul order.

385. Dreamed I was sneaking off with my sister to have sex.

386. Dreamed I was in a giant apartment complex owned by my father, I went into someone's room and stole something.

387. Dreamed I kissed a girl on Facebook I know called Gloria Asmodeus. She was shorter than I thought she would be. Then someone knocked on the door asking directions to somewhere.

388. Dreamed about my ex girlfriend D. We cuddled kissed and made

out. Then she left to go somewhere and left her phone behind, I couldn't stop my curiosity and looked through it. Sure enough she had several boyfriends.

389. Dreamed I was lying in a room of my house with my head resting on one of my rolled up carpets that has a goetia circle on it. I was talking to my sister about the magic a person can do when they learn to control the vibratory tones in their voice. Some one came into the house and tried to steal one of the magic circles but I stopped them.

390. Dreamed I was having a band meeting with Chad Terry there. I was discussing the possibility of Chad taking up the vocals again and me playing bass guitar.

391. Dreamed I received a message file on my computer that showed my ex girlfriend D posing nude, sucking dick, and lying on a bed naked with other naked people.

392. Dreamed I ran into Cassie, the ex girlfriend of my friend Cliff. Cassie and I cuddled like lovers it was very nice, and seemed very real.

393. Dreamed I was at a house where Natalie, Christina, and Jeremy, my old friends were. We talked like it was old times.

394. Dreamed junkie Cliff came to the house. We were talking about various things and I was both happy and angry with him.

395. Dreamed this half retarded village idiot guy from my neighborhood was at my house, he was high on dope, out of his mind and babbling about various things. I tried to get him to leave my house but he was so high he couldn't understand me.

396. Dreamed I was hanging out with Kavita Rita, she was hanging on me and being all sweet and her energy felt good.

397. Dreamed there was a copy of the magic book called "the sacred magic of abramelin" on my desk with candles lit around it and a mysterious vibe in the air. Suddenly I was startled by the appearance of my ex girlfriend Chevelle. She seemed to radiate a strange power and her hair was a darker red than usual. I took a deep breath and told her that she was crazy and that she might burn my house down leaving candles burning like that.

398. Dreamed I was at a long and boring church service at my moms church. Finally I left the upstairs during the middle of a cringe worthy sermon and wandered downstairs. There was a dinner being prepared. I remember thinking "I hate this, I am x number of years old, and I am still at this church, I have tried to escape this place so many times, will I ever get free of these people?"

399. Dreamed I was in the middle of a drug deal at my house and my mom showed up unannounced. I simply refused to tell her what was going on.

400. Dreamed a long dream about Will P. There were many strange and out of place details. He had a new baby, a bunch of bass guitars in his closet, etc. My ex girlfriend Chevelle arrived and her and I worked things out.

401. Dreamed I was taking to Derrick about Megan P.

402. Dreamed I was at moms church and there was a heavy set black preacher there that was famous and I had heard his voice on the radio before. I was in the foyer listening because I couldn't stand to be in the

sanctuary of the church.

403. Dreamed I was at Missouri Southern State University with my ex girlfriend D. We went off in the woods to have sex on a blanket.

404. (flying dream number 57) Dreamed I was fighting with my brother Amiel. I was flying, and punching and kicking, throwing things and breaking glass. This seemed to go on for hours, from scene to scene.

405. Dreamed Natalie and Scott were here at my house. I heard them come in and strangely, I was in bed when they did. I sat up and had a conversation with them from upstairs, while they were downstairs. Before this I had been dreaming of working on a band project.

406. Dreamed a crazy nightmare dream where me and another man were trying to transport my sister through a darkened city. Then after we had accomplished this task we learned there was some sort of evil serial rapist who had kidnapped a young girl and chained her up in his house. Me and a couple other guys were desperately trying to find him and destroy him for his actions and free the girl.

407. (flying dream number 58) Dreamed a long dream about the church of Satan. I was helping to build a physical church and working on the framing of it. There was a bunch of people there who knew me. Zena Schreck, the daughter of Anton Lavey was there. Her and I were fighting against some powerful flying vampires. I flew carrying Zena, but I couldn't fly very far with the effort of carrying her, I landed in a darkly lit courtyard and set her down and by that time the vampires were upon us. Her and I fought them with knives in our hands and one of them lost his head in the fight. The strange thing was that I had dreamed the whole dream before.

408. Dreamed I was talking to my father, and I knew that I was dreaming and simply accepted that I was talking to his ghost. He also knew he was dead. He told me that my mom complains to him in dreams about her new husband and I smiled and made a joke saying that her new husband complains to me about mom.

409. Dreamed me and another person were hanging out with some rich person in a well furnished home. The rich people were listening to a grungy rockabilly style song. But I felt out of place because they were so rich.

410. Dreamed I was putting together a new band and there were a lot of different musicians there trying out for the band. Pete Altendorf was there and finally the musicians got a song together and we started playing it and the music was great.

411. Dreamed me and my sister were playing around sexually. She stopped and wandered off and I wanted to keep going. My mother came up suddenly and asked why my sister was upset, I shrugged and said I did not know. Then the scene changed from my parents old farm to a new house dad had bought at a different location. I watched my dad organize his new shop for a while with a strange feeling about me. Everything seemed familiar, yet something was out of place and I couldn't tell what it was. There were several all terrain vehicles there and I was going to take some kids for a ride on one of them but there was too much mud after a rain.

412. Dreamed I was at my moms old house, my mom was there and made a deal for me to do some painting, I felt like I did not trust my mom, and that she had some motive for what she was offering me, but I was happy to have the opportunity to make some money.

413. Dreamed a long dream about datura, there were big bags of the

prickly seed pods. I was allowed to take some of them to plant, and I stuffed several glass jars with the seed pods for later. There was a redhaired woman there that was very calm, beautiful, and earthy. We were going to have a child together. I think this may have been a plant spirit, the so called "Lady Datura".

414. Dreamed I saw the blue truck I sold to Cliff parked somewhere with no one in it. I thought, "well I guess he lost his truck".

415. Dreamed I was at moms church playing some kind of game like "hide and seek".

416. Dreamed I was at an amusement park or carnival of some kind and it was night. I was talking to some guy about demonology. A girl I know from Facebook walked up to us, and because of the subject of the conversation he got quiet suddenly. I said "oh, don't worry, she knows about Asmodeus".

417. Dreamed I was down at my neighbor house, the one who is nicknamed "wormy". I had sex in the back room with a young, but legal girl, meanwhile wormy had sex in the front room with a willing, but underage teenager.

418. Dreamed about a guy I only know on Facebook. He is a Satanist and overall shady character named Ty Dawson. We were hanging out and talking somewhere and I wanted to demonstrate to him my magical powers so I got up close to him and then backed away from him with magical speed.

419. Dreamed about fingering my sister's pussy and wanting to sneak off somewhere with her to have sex.

420. (flying dream number 59) Dreamed I was near a large pond and I was flying over the water, as I looked down into the water I saw many snakes swimming in groups in the water. I flew too close to the water and one of the snakes came up out of the water and bit me. There were people on the bank of the pond watching me fly.

421. (flying dream number 60) Dreamed I was somewhere hanging out with my ex girlfriend D. She did something I did not approve of and I left her to go flying. I flee around for a while and then was suddenly in the bedroom I grew up in of the trailer in my family farm. For some reason I believed that I was not dreaming, and that I really could fly, it took a lot of effort to fly, and I was sort of swimming through the air but I could do it.

422. Dreamed I was in the sound booth at a radio station, about to be interviewed for a radio show on the occult.

423. Dreamed I saw my mother without a shirt on and her tits were sagging. She looked at me sadly and said "a womans beauty fades".

424. Dreamed a beautiful redheaded girl wanted to be my girlfriend.

425. Dreamed I found a large crystal on the ground. It was very clear and good quality.

426. (flying dream 61) Dreamed I was flying but I could not fly very well.

427. Dreamed I was talking to Frater Ashen Chassan about magic.

428. Dreamed I was at a darkly lit slaughter house for cows, I was moving around very fast, by using my magic wand to sort of pole vault

over things or spring along the ground. I was disgusted by the place, there was a huge shower that washed the blood off of the machinery after it was used to cut apart a cow.

429. Dreamed I was looking at two different versions of the hexagram of Solomon from the goetia. One of them was red and the other was in the traditional colors. I had created both of them in the past.

430. Dreamed my ex girlfriend D had a new boyfriend, he was Russian or something like that.

431. Dreamed I saw Will P and greeted him warmly. I was happy to see him.

432. Dreamed I saw my ex girlfriend Tracy and she had cut her long red hair short up to her shoulders.

433. Dreamed I was going to be a long haul trucker and drive a semi across America. My mom was talking to me before I left in my first drive and she was worried. I said to her "if I die, that's ok, I have lived a good life."

434. Dreamed I was standing in a room, the fitness instructor named Shaun T from the workout videos I do was there having sex with a very fit south american woman. They were covered in sweat and not paying any attention to me at all. His penis was huge and thrusting in and out of the woman and they were smiling and laughing and having a good time. They seemed very relaxed.

435. (Flying dream number 62) Dreamed I was flying in a large room. My ability to fly was like never before in any dream, it seemed effortless, I could soar high up in the air and then make big dives in a

circle.

436. Dreamed I was playing with a real samurai or ninja sword, practicing techniques I had learned from ninjutsu. Careful because the sword was sharp.

437. Dreamed a long dream where I was with my ex girlfriend D and we were at my parents church and we ate some acid. After that we were driving around and somehow ended up at a party at my brothers house. D and I got separated and she picked up a couple of Mexican boys who were following her around trying to fuck her. This annoyed me and I somehow chased them off. Then D and I went wandering around a variety of strange locations including a yoga school that had an entrance to it that was also a shower and seemed to be from the future. We seemed to be in a different place each time we went into a different room. It was like I was dreaming inside her mind, or we were both creating the dream together. I just wanted to get her out of there and back to my place but we could not find her car. Right when my confusion and stress reached it's peak, I was suddenly wide awake in my bed.

438. Dreamed my shoes were wearing out and I was stressed out about it.

439. (flying dream number 63) Dreamed I was living in a high rise apt. My ex girlfriend D was there asleep upstairs. My ex girlfriend Chevelle came over and started talking to me. When she found out D was there she became very angry and started chasing me up and down the stairs except I was flying. I thought it was funny that she was angry and so my ability to fly was very good, I flee ahead of her taunting her.

440. Dreamed Barton Drake, the son of my witch friend Lana, was at the door of my house. It seemed so damn real, very clear, bright colors.

441. Dreamed I saw my ex wife Kyleen, she looked beautiful and happy and healthy.

442. Dreamed I saw Jess Johnson, my drummer in an old band. He was walking down a street as I was driving by him. He looked happy and at peace.

Note: it was about this time that I began to try a very special experiment. I determined that I could program myself to dream of girl I had met on the internet named Simona L. My method of doing this was to say to myself every night upon going to sleep, "tonight I will dream of Simona!" I began to do this at this point.

443. Dreamed I was in a personal duel of honor with another male. For some reason I had been told he was looking to beat me up and I was scared and carrying around a shovel as a weapon. The I saw the guy, he looked like the boyfriend of a girl I had been flirting with on Facebook named Simona L, although at the moment I didn't think of this. I was overcome by a feeling of rage and threw down the shovel and screamed at him "I will beat you with my bare hands!"

444. Dreamed I was excitedly telling someone I had quit smoking.

445. Dreamed I had a long coversation with a magician I only know on Facebook and have never spoken to. His name is Kurtis Joseph. He was very articulate and we spoke on about various branches of magic. Very cool guy, and His work was interesting.

446. (flying dream number 64) Dreamed I was showing my dad that I could fly by breathing in and then pushing energy out of my base chakra. For a moment, I realized I was dreaming.

447. Dreamed something about 3000 dollars, getting it, spending it, idk.

448. Dreamed I was talking to a girl about sex.

449. Dreamed I was having a conversation with a girl about sex, the same girl as the previous night.

450. Dreamed I was talking to a girl and the last thing I said to her was an expression from Thelema. I said "93 sister" then I woke up.

451. Dreamed I had looked at Facebook for so long I saw everything there was to see.

452. Dreamed I completed the tools and equipment for the traditional goetia work of calling up demons.

453. Dreamed I was out at the old family farm. Each of my family members was working on different jobs my dad had given them. My brother Amiels job was easy and he was getting fat and lazy.

454. Dreamed I was playing with a racoon and petting it like a cat. We were very close and there was a strong bond of energy between us. I believe it was the ghost of the racoon whose skin is a part of my goetia evocation tools.

455. (flying dream number 65) Dreamed a long flying dream where my mom and sister were watching me fly and I was very high up in the sky.

456. Dreamed my dad caught me growing some drugs and stole them from me.

457. Dreamed I was out in my yard and almost stepped on a snake.

458. Dreamed I was living with my dad and couldn't find my bedroom. My aunt Sharon lived there as well.

459. Dreamed I was having a long conversation with someone about the Al Ghoul order and the difference between it and the Dragon Rouge order.

460. Dreamed I was learning about the shamanic concept of the assembly point described by Carlos Castaneda. I woke up briefly and decided I wanted to go back into the dream. So I simply stopped talking to myself and silenced my mind. Immediately I went back into the same dream I had just been having. I found myself standing at the top of an area where there were two staircases leading downward, side by side but to different rooms.

461. Dreamed I was at a shopping mall, the strange thing was, I had been there before, but only in dreams.

462. Dreamed I was in my room in a house I had lived in before. My room was on the third floor. I had only been there before in other dreams. This is the second night in a row that I had been to a place that was familiar to me because I had been there before in other dreams.

463. Dreamed I was watching an infant child and my mother and sister came and took it away from me.

464. Dreamed my ex girlfriend D came to my bed and wanted to cuddle. I said to her "what about all the awful things you did to me"? She apologized and then we cuddled and went to sleep.

465. Dreamed I was a little baby and Ashley was my mother. She was sleeping nearly naked on a bed and I couldn't reach her to wake her up.

466. Dreamed me and another friend ran into several teenage girls that started kissing us and it was incredibly hot.

467. Dreamed my aunt Sharon was younger and moving around with more agility than she does now.

468. Dreamed of Amos the billy goat that my neighbor owns. I was in his yard playing with the goat.

469. Dreamed I was walking down an escalator in a strange city. There were people all around me that seemed to be dressed in a European manner. I saw a pretty girl come down the escalator in a hurry. I looked over at her and thought "that looks like Simona L". She stopped and looked up at me. Suddenly I knew it was Simona. I couldn't believe my eyes. I said "Simona is that really you"? It was. We stopped moving right there on the escalator and she touched my hand and there was energy that passed between us very strong, but we did not share more than touching hands because we both knew that her boyfriend was around somewhere nearby. We then moved down the escalator to a place where there were doors leading in different directions. Simona said she had to go to work and I would see her later and passed through one of the doors. I wandered around the building for some time feeling high on the energy we had exchanged. I later found myself at the top of the stairs again sitting at a small round table by a vending machine. There was a pencil and paper In front of me and I was trying to finish a test of some kind. Simona came back and her boyfriend was with her. It was getting late in the evening and I was going to go to their house to stay overnight as soon as I was done with the test. (this completed my experiment to find Simona in dreaming)

470. Dreamed I had sex with three different teenage girls, and proudly bragged to my older brother about it.

471. (flying dream number 66) Dreamed I was flying around some familiar area, it seemed to be the old family recycling business.

472. Dreamed about finding a magical rams horn trumpet called a shofar.

473. Dreamed about talking to Kevin Williams, the old bass player for the band Frail.

474. Dreamed my ex girlfriend D and I were hanging out, her ex boyfriend came over and they started having sex even though I was there and I was outraged.

475. Dreamed something terrible happened to Ashley and one of her kids.

476. (flying dream number 67) Dreamed I was at my moms church and started feeling bored and trapped as usual. I decided to climb up on the roof and jump off it to try and fly. As I was climbing up on the roof a little kid spotted me and said it was going to tell my mom on me. I said "no! Don't tell her, she hates it when I fly". I did climb up and jumped off of the roof and flew in a gliding motion about 70 feet.

477. Dreamed I was a kid again and was playing with other kids and everything seemed simple and fun.

478. Dreamed my ex girlfriend D was here. We had a long talk that went nowhere. She wanted me to financially support her, but she also wanted to continue to live with her mother. I didn't trust her to be

faithful to me and had no desire to support her unless she was.

479. (flying dream number 6s) Dreamed I was flying at an old theatre. It seemed like a place I have been several times in dreams. It seems so familiar but it is not a place I know in the physical world.

480. (flying dream number 69) Dreamed I was flying around at my parents old farm, it was a bright clear day in the summer And I would drop down to the ground and walk through the brushes for a while and then fly up and move around in the air just above the trees for a while.

481. Dreamed I suddenly realized my mother was on my chest with both her knees pressed against me. I found this very uncomfortable and thought "What the hell"? I told her to get off of me and she kept talking about the same stuff she always does, religion this, I am a sinner who need to dedicate my life to her form of God etc. I tried to reason with her for some time but she was almost hysterical and going around in circles with her words. I finally said I was tired of listening to her "stupid ignorant bullshit" and told her if she didn't get off of my chest I was going to grab her by the throat. Suddenly I noticed my dad was lying on the bed beside me and I turned my head to look at him and said "if she doesn't get off of me I am going to grab her by the throat!" He seemed unconcerned by this and finally I lost all patience and grabbed my mother by the throat. It was at that moment that I woke up.

482. Dreamed I argued with my ex girlfriend D for what seemed like hours. She kept trying to win the argument by getting me angry or confusing me or talking in circles. I was on to her games though and so she got nowhere with those tricks. Finally at the end of all that she we had sex, simply because she wanted to do so as a way for her to feel that she had won the argument.

Made in the USA
Coppell, TX
04 December 2021

67115011R00049